Bernice

by Thornton Wilder

A Samuel French Acting Edition

SAMUELFRENCH.COM

Copyright © 1957, 1961
Yale University, Fisk University and Oberlin College.
Foreword copyright © 2014 by Tappan Wilder
All Rights Reserved

BERNICE is fully protected under the copyright laws of the United States of America and all countries with which the United States has reciprocal copyright relations, whether through bilateral or multi-lateral treaties or otherwise, and including but not limited to, all countries covered by the Pan-American Copyright Convention, the Universal Copyright Convention, and the Berne Convention. All rights, including professional and amateur stage productions, recitation, lecturing, public reading, motion picture, radio broadcasting, television and the rights of translation into foreign languages are strictly reserved.

ISBN 978-0-573-70387-4

www.SamuelFrench.com
www.SamuelFrench-London.co.uk

For Production Enquiries

United States and Canada
Info@SamuelFrench.com
1-866-598-8449

Amateur Rights in the United Kingdom
Plays@SamuelFrench-London.co.uk
020-7255-4302

Each title is subject to availability from Samuel French, depending upon country of performance. Please be aware that *BERNICE* may not be licensed by Samuel French in your territory. Producers should contact the nearest Samuel French office or licensing partner to verify availability.

For all enquiries regarding Professional productions in the United Kingdom; Professional and Amateur productions throughout the rest of Europe; and motion picture, television, and other media rights, please contact Alan Brodie Representation (Victoria@AlanBrodie.com). Visit www.thorntonwilder.com/contact for details.

CAUTION: Professional and amateur producers are hereby warned that *BERNICE* is subject to a licensing fee. Publication of this play does not imply availability for performance. Professionals and Amateurs considering a production are strongly advised to apply for a license before starting rehearsals, advertising, or booking a theatre. A licensing fee must be paid whether the title is presented for charity or gain and whether or not admission is charged.

No one shall make any changes in this title for the purpose of production. No part of this book may be reproduced, stored in a retrieval system, or transmitted in any form, by any means, now known or yet to be invented, including mechanical, electronic, photocopying, recording, videotaping, or otherwise, without the prior written permission of the publisher. No one shall upload this title, or part of this title, to any social media websites.

MUSIC USE NOTE

Licensees are solely responsible for obtaining formal written permission from copyright owners to use copyrighted music in the performance of this play and are strongly cautioned to do so. If no such permission is obtained by the licensee, then the licensee must use only original music that the licensee owns and controls. Licensees are solely responsible and liable for all music clearances and shall indemnify the copyright owners of the play and their licensing agent, Samuel French, against any costs, expenses, losses and liabilities arising from the use of music by licensees. Please contact the appropriate music licensing authority in your territory for the rights to any incidental music.

IMPORTANT BILLING AND CREDIT REQUIREMENTS

All producers of *BERNICE* must give credit to the author of the play in all programs distributed in connection with performances of the play, and in all instances in which the title of the play appears for the purposes of advertising, publicizing or otherwise exploiting the play and/or a production. The name of the author must appear on a separate line on which no other name appears, immediately following the title and must appear in size of type not less than fifty percent of the size of the title type.

> This play may be performed only in its entirety. No permission can be granted for cuttings, readings or any use of parts of the play for any purpose whatsoever without the express written permission of the Wilder Family LLC. Absolutely *no* changes can be made to the text.

INTRODUCTION TO WILDER'S *BERNICE*
THE SIN OF PRIDE

From the time he began dreaming up plays as a boy Thornton Wilder's vision of the theater transcended conventional boundaries, and to the end of his life his vision continually evolved and expanded. In 1956, he began work on what grew into an extravagantly ambitious project: two cycles of seven one-act plays based on the Deadly Sins and the Ages of Man. *Bernice* represents "Pride" in Wilder's projected cycle on the Seven Deadly Sins.

In what would prove to be his final dramatic works, Wilder sought not only to explore the theatrical possibilities inherent in the Sins and Ages, but (as he phrased it in his private journal on Christmas Day 1960) to "offer each play in the series as representing, also, a different mode of playwriting: Grand Guignol, Chekhov, Noh play, etc., etc." In short, he envisioned nothing less than a *tour de force* of dramatic theme and form encapsulated in the economy and intensity of the one-act play.

Wilder did not complete the challenge he set for himself, but he came close. The surviving work enriches his dramatic legacy and deserves to be remembered as more than a footnote to his lifelong conviction (written soon after *Our Town* opened on Broadway in 1938): "The theater offers to imaginative narration its highest possibilities."

THE SINS AND AGES THEN AND NOW

A brief overview of the history of these plays will help readers place them in Wilder's career as a dramatist. Two Sins, *Bernice* (Pride) and *The Wreck on the 5:25* (Sloth), premiered in English at a special event in Berlin in 1957 (with Wilder performing in *Bernice*). For reasons that have never been clear, for he enjoyed the experience and felt that plays did well, he withdrew them. That same year a third Sin, *The Drunken Sisters* (Gluttony), written as the satyr play for Wilder's full length drama, *The Alcestiad*, proved successful in its premiere on the stage of Zürich's fabled Schauspielhaus.

Five years passed before the continuation of his ambitious scheme appeared on a stage in the United States. In January 1962, two new Ages (*Infancy* and *Childhood*) and a new Sin, *Someone From Assisi* (Lust), opened at Circle in the Square, then located off-Broadway on Bleecker Street, to the reported largest pre-opening advanced sale in that stage's then 11-year history. Billed as "Plays for Bleecker Street," the show of ran for 349 performances.

Then silence. After "Plays for Bleecker Street" closed, no more Sins or Ages appeared. When Thornton Wilder died in 1975 the public record of his 14-play scheme contained only four plays – two Ages (*Infancy* and *Childhood*) and two Sins (Lust and Gluttony).

Today, eleven of Wilder's Sins and Ages are available for production: a completed cycle of the seven Deadly Sins and four of seven Ages of Man. The source of the seven "new" plays is no secret. The missing pieces were found in Thornton Wilder's archives at Yale[1]. From this source, starting in 1995, his literary executor and family released the two plays withdrawn in 1957, *Cement Hands* (Avarice), and four additional titles (*Youth, The Rivers Under the Earth* [Middle Age][2], *A Ringing of Doorbells* [Envy] and *In Shakespeare and the Bible* [Wrath]) recovered and completed by the actor, director and friend of Wilder's, F.J. O'Neil. (Mr. O'Neil's valuable notes on the origin of each of these missing links follow the text of each play.)

The public reception of Thornton Wilder's long lost and new plays was gratifying. *The Wreck on the 5:25* was selected as one of the Best American Short Plays of 1994-95. In 1997, the Centenary of the playwright's birth, Kevin Kline starred in a premiere reading in New York of *Cement Hands*, and the works recovered by Mr. O'Neil served as the centerpieces of Actors Theatre of Louisville's 13th Annual Brown-Forman Classics in Context Festival. Finally, as the capstone to the Centenary celebration, TCG Press in 1997 published the 11 Sins and Ages in Volume I of *The Collected Short Plays of Thornton Wilder*.

---

[1] No additional one-acts remain to be discovered in Thornton Wilder's archives at Yale.

[2] We believe Wilder intended *The Rivers Under the Earth* to represent Middle Age.

Wilder never followed conventional theatrical practice. As a young writer in his "Classic One Act Plays" of 1931, he swept away scenery and played provocative games with time and place. In the Sins and Ages, his farewell as a playwright, he is no less adventurous by way of settings, techniques, stage-craft and themes. One artistic trend of the day especially "fired his imagination" where these plays are concerned: his passionate belief in the value of the arena stage. "The boxed set play," he wrote in 1961, "encourages the anecdote…The unencumbered stage encourages the truth in everyone." Wilder felt so strongly that audiences should be seated as close to the actors as possible that Samuel French, for several years, was only permitted to license these plays to companies agreeing to perform them on a three-sided thrust or arena stage.

***

As part of its celebration of Wilder's one-act plays, Samuel French and the Wilder family take great pleasure in issuing new acting editions for the Sins and Ages long in print and, for the first time, acting editions of the seven new Wilder works. We invite those performing or teaching these plays to visit www.thorntonwilder.com for additional information.

– *Tappan Wilder,*
Literary Executor for Thornton Wilder

CHARACTERS

MR. MALLISON, Mr. Walbeck's lawyer, fifty-nine
BERNICE MAYHEW, Mr. Walbeck's maid, fifty
THE DRIVER
MR. WALBECK, forty-seven

SETTING

Drawing room of a house in Chicago, 1911.

(Door into the hall at the back. All we need see are an elaborate, but not weighty, table in the center and two chairs. At the front of the stage are some andirons and a poker, indicating a fireplace. **MALLISON**, *fifty-nine, all a lawyer, now very nervous, is standing before the table holding an open watch in his hand. By the door is* **BERNICE**, *colored, fifty, in a maid's uniform.)*

MALLISON. Remind me…remind me, please…your name?

BERNICE. *(unimpressed)* Bernice.

MALLISON. Thank you. – Now Mr. Burgess, your employer, may be a little bit…moody. You do whatever he wants. Have you enough help to run the house?

BERNICE. I did what you told me. There's Jason for the heavy work and the furnace. This Mr. Burgess – will he be alone in this house?

MALLISON. Alone? Oh! Most probably. At all events, you are in charge. Get whatever help you need. I am Mr. Burgess's lawyer, but he will be getting another lawyer soon. All your bills will be paid, I'm sure…You have some dinner waiting for him now?

BERNICE. *(slowly)* Why do you talk so funny about this Mr. Burgess? Is he coming from the crazy house or something?

MALLISON. *(outraged)* No, indeed!! I don't know where you got such an idea. All that's expected of you is…uh… good meals and a well-run house.

BERNICE. You talk very funny, Mr. Mallison.

MALLISON. *(after swallowing with dignity and glaring at her)* Mrs. Willard recommended you as an experienced cook and housekeeper, Bernice. My duty ends there.

BERNICE. I don't have to take any jobs unless I likes them, Mr. Mallison. I never agrees to work any place more than three days. Mrs. Willard don't like it, but that's my terms – if I likes it, I stays.

MALLISON. Well, I hope you like it here. You're getting very well paid and you can ask for any further help you need – within reason. There's an automobile stopping before the door now. I think you'd better go to the door.

(**BERNICE** *doesn't move. Arms akimbo, she looks musingly at* **MALLISON**.)

BERNICE. I seen people like you before…You're up to something.

(The front door bell rings.)

MALLISON. I don't like your tone. You've been engaged to work here – for three days, anyway. You can begin by answering that door bell.

(**BERNICE** *goes out.* **MALLISON** *straightens his clothes, goes to the table and picks up his briefcase, then stands waiting with pursed lips. Sounds of altercation from the hall.*)

DRIVER'S VOICE. All right! The price is twenty dollars. But if I'd know'd it was a night like this –

(Enter the **DRIVER**, *a livery stable chauffeur, Irish, slightly drunk. He is carrying a small rattan suitcase, which he puts down by the door. He is followed by* **WALBECK**, *forty-seven, prematurely gray; he speaks softly, but gives an impression of controlled power.* **BERNICE** *enters behind them.*)

WALBECK. *(to* **MALLISON**, *in a low voice)* I understood that the fare was paid in advance?

MALLISON. The twenty dollars was paid in advance.

DRIVER. Anybody'd charge twice to drive on a night like this. First it was rain and snow –

MALLISON. The livery stable was given twenty dollars – *(to* **BERNICE***)* You can prepare the dinner!

(exit **BERNICE***)*

DRIVER. Then it turned to ice. The worst night I've ever seen, to go to Joliet and pick up a I-don't-know-what. The car falling off the road every minute. To go to Joliet and pick up a criminal of some sort –

WALBECK. *(gesture of empty pockets)* I have no money.

MALLISON. *(to the* **DRIVER***)* I will give you five dollars, but I shall report you to the livery stable.

DRIVER. *(taking the bill)* What do I care? Thirty-five miles each way and half the time you couldn't see the road five yards in front of you; and the other half sliding into the ditch. All right, tell 'em and see what I tell 'em.

MALLISON. You have your five dollars. If you go now, I'll say nothing to your superiors – But go!

DRIVER. *(starting for the door, then turning on* **WALBECK***)* And who do you think you are, Mr. Bur-gessss! Keeping your mouth so shut! You a murderer or I-don't-know-what; and too big and mighty to talk to anybody. – Oh, you had to think, did you? So you had to think? Well, you've got enough to think about for the rest of your goddamned life.

(He goes out.)

MALLISON. *(stiffly)* Good evening, Mr. Walbeck.

(The front door is heard closing with a slam.)

WALBECK. *(always softly, but impersonally)* What is this name of…Burgess?

MALLISON. We assumed, Mr. Walbeck, that you would prefer us to engage the household staff and…make certain other arrangements under…another name. Since you did not reply to our letters on this matter, we selected the name of Burgess.

WALBECK. I see. – Is…my wife here?

MALLISON. *(astonished)* You did not get Mrs. Walbeck's letters?

WALBECK. I did not open any letters.

MALLISON. And our letters, Mr. Walbeck?

WALBECK. I haven't opened any letters for six months.

MALLISON. *(controlling his outrage, primly)* Mrs. Walbeck left a week ago – with the children – for California. She has filed a petition for divorce. In her letters she probably explained it to you at length. She did not wish to make this move earlier…She wished it to be known that she stood by you through…your ordeal. When she heard that your sentence had been reduced and that you would be returning this week, she –

WALBECK. *(coolly)* There's no need to say anything more, Mr. Mallison.

MALLISON. A woman has been engaged to attend to your needs. Her name is Bernice. A wardrobe – that is, a wardrobe of clothes – you will find upstairs. Your measurements were obtained by your former tailor from the authorities at the…institution from which you have come. – Here are the keys of the house. Here are the statements from your bank. A checkbook. Here *(He places a long envelope on the table.)* are five hundred dollars which I have drawn for your immediate needs.

WALBECK. Thank you. Good night.

MALLISON. Mr. Walbeck, hitherto the firm of Bremerton, Bremerton, Mallison and Mallison has been happy to serve as your legal representatives. From now on we trust that you will find other counsel. We relinquish – here *(He lays down another document.)* our power of attorney. And in this envelope you will find all the documents and information that our successors will require. I wish you good night.

WALBECK. *(stonily)* Good night.

(MALLISON turns at the door.)

MALLISON. You read no letters?

WALBECK. *(his eyes on the ground)* No.

MALLISON. That reminds me. Your daughter Lavinia wished to leave a letter for you. Her mother forbade her to do so. However, I…I was prepared to take the responsibility. Your daughter gave me this letter to give to you.

(He gives an envelope to **WALBECK**, *who puts it in his breast pocket. His silence and level glance complete* **MALLISON***'s discomfiture.)*

MALLISON. *(cont.)* Good night, sir.

(Exit **MALLISON**. **WALBECK** *stands motionless gazing fixedly before him. Suddenly, in a rage, he overturns the table before him; but immediately recovers his self-control. Enter* **BERNICE***.)*

BERNICE. Dinner's served, sir.

WALBECK. I won't have any dinner.

BERNICE. Yes, Mr. Burgess.

WALBECK. What?

BERNICE. I said, "Yes, Mr. Burgess." I'll just set that table to rights.

WALBECK. *(quickly)* I'll do it.

(He does.)

BERNICE. *(watchfully but unsentimentally)* I've got a real good steak in there. I'm the best cook in Chicago, Mr. Burgess. There's lots of people that knows that.

WALBECK. Is there any liquor in the house?

BERNICE. Oh, yes. There's everything.

WALBECK. Rye. Rye straight. – You eat the steak.

BERNICE. Thank you, Mr. Burgess. *(She starts out, then turns.)* Now, you don't want to eat that steak, Mr. Burgess, but I've got some tomato soup there that's the best tomato soup you ever ate. You aren't going to waste my time by refusing to eat that soup.

WALBECK. *(looking at her; impersonally)* What is your name?

BERNICE. My name's Bernice Mayhew. People calls me Bernice.

WALBECK. Bernice, I don't want to eat in that dining room. You can bring me the rye and some of that soup in here.

BERNICE. Yes, Mr. Burgess.

WALBECK. My name is Walbeck.

BERNICE. What's that?

WALBECK. My name: Wal-beck, Walbeck.

BERNICE. Yes, Mr. Walbeck.

WALBECK. And pour yourself some rye, Bernice.

BERNICE. I don't touch it, Mr. Walbeck. Ten years ago I made my life over. I changed my name and I changed everything about myself. I thank you, but I don't touch liquor.

(She goes out. **WALBECK**, *standing straight, his eyes on the ground, puts his hand in his pocket and draws out his daughter's letter. After a moment's hesitation, he opens it. He holds it suspended in his hand a moment. Then he tears the letter and envelope, each two ways, and throws the fragments into the fire [invisible to us], between the andirons.* **BERNICE** *returns, pushing a small service table. She gives him the rye, then unfurls a tablecloth and starts laying the table.* **WALBECK** *drinks half the rye in one swallow.)*

WALBECK. Were you here when my wife was here?

BERNICE. No, sir. Nobody's been here today but that lawyer-man. I came here this morning and all day Jason and I have been cleaning the house.

WALBECK. Do you know where I come from?

BERNICE. *(quietly, lowered eye)* Yes, I do.

WALBECK. Did that lawyer tell you?

BERNICE. No…I knew…I been there myself…So I knew. I'll get your soup.

(She goes out. Suddenly **WALBECK** *goes to the fireplace. Falling on his knees, he tries without burning his fingers to rake out the fragments of the letter. Apparently it is too late.* **BERNICE** *enters with a covered soup tureen. Watchfully, but with no show of surprise, she tries to take in what he is doing.* **WALBECK** *rises, dusting off his knees.)*

You want me to build up that fire, Mr. Walbeck?

WALBECK. No, it's all right as it is.

(He seats himself at the table.)

BERNICE. *(eyeing the fireplace speculatively)* There's some toast there, too.

WALBECK. You say you changed your name?

BERNICE. Yes. My born name was Sarah Temple. When I came out of prison I was Bernice Mayhew. Of course, I had some other names too. I was married twice. But Bernice Mayhew was the name I gave myself. *(without emphasis; her eyes on the distance)* I was in because I killed somebody.

WALBECK. *(the soup spoon at his mouth, speaks in her tone)* I was in because I cheated two or three hundred people out of money.

BERNICE. *(musingly)* Well, everybody's done something.

(Pause. **WALBECK** *eats.)*

WALBECK. You say you changed everything about yourself?

BERNICE. Yes. Everything was changed, anyway. I was in a disgrace – nobody can be in a bigger disgrace than I was. And some people were avoiding me and some people were laughing at me and some people were being kind to me, like I was a dog that came to the back door. And some people were saying cheer up, Sarah, you've paid your price. There's lots of things to live for. You're young yet. – You're sure you wouldn't like a piece of that steak, Mr. Walbeck, rare or any way you'd like it?

WALBECK. No. I'm going downtown soon. If I get hungry, later, I'll pick up something to eat down there.

BERNICE. *(after a short pause, while she continues to gaze into the distance)* Did anybody come to meet you when you came out of the door of the place you was at?

WALBECK. No.

BERNICE. That's what I mean. I don't blame them. I wouldn't want to go 'round with a person who's very much in a disgrace – like with a person who's killed somebody. I wouldn't choose 'em.

WALBECK. Or with a person who's stolen a lot of people's life savings.

BERNICE. I only mentioned that to show a big part of the change: you're alone.

WALBECK. Did that lawyer who was here, or the agency, know that you'd been in prison?

BERNICE. Oh, no. It was Sarah Temple who did that. She's dead. When I changed my name she became dead. You see the first part of my life I lived in Kansas City. Then I came to Chicago. Bernice Mayhew has never been to Kansas City. She don't even know what it looks like.

WALBECK. *(impersonally, without looking at her)* If you've been on your feet all day cleaning the house, I think you'd better sit down, Bernice.

BERNICE. Well, thank you, I will sit down.

WALBECK. Would you advise me to kill off George Walbeck?

BERNICE. *(seeming more and more remote, in her musings)* Not so much for your sake as for other people's sake. It's not good for other people to have to do with persons who are in a disgrace; it brings out the worst in them. I don't like to see that.

WALBECK. *(slowly, his eyes on the distance)* I guess you're right. I'd better do that.

BERNICE. It's like what happens about poor people. You're a thousand times richer than I am, but I'm richer than millions of people. What good does it do to think about them? I only need one real meal a day; the rest is just stuffing. But I don't notice as how I give up my other two meals. I'm always right there at mealtimes. When I went hungry, most times I didn't let people know about it; and when I'm in a disgrace, why should I make them uncomfortable?

WALBECK. Before you became Bernice Mayhew, did you have any children?

BERNICE. Yes, I did…Their mother's dead, of course. But I guess somebody's reminding them every day that their mother was a murderer. – That's bad enough, but it's not as bad as knowing their mother's alive. – Have you noticed that we gradually forgive them that's dead? If I was alive they'd be thinking about me, in one way or another hating me or maybe trying to stand up for me. There are a lot of ideas young people could go through about a thing like that.

WALBECK. *(as though to himself)* Yes.

(The telephone rings in the hall. **WALBECK** *rises uneasily.)*

Who could that be? Answer it, will you, Bernice? Don't say that I'm here.

*(***BERNICE** *goes into the hall. Her voice can be heard shouting as though she were unaccustomed to the telephone.)*

BERNICE. It's me talking – Bernice. Yes. Who are you, talking? Who? Oh. I can't understand much. A letter? I hear you, a letter. Yes, miss. What? I can't hear good. The machine don't work good. All right, you come. I'm here. Bernice. Yes, you come. I'm here.

*(***BERNICE** *returns to the stage.)*

She says she's your daughter.

WALBECK. So-o-o! She didn't go to California with her mother.

BERNICE. She says she sent you a letter. In the letter she asked you to telephone her…that she could come and see you. She was asking over and over again if you was here, but I made out that the machine didn't work good. She says she'll be here soon.

*(***BERNICE** *has been clearing the table, putting the objects on the wheeled service table, which she starts pushing to the door.)*

WALBECK. I can't see her tonight. – What do you suppose she wants?

BERNICE. *(at the door with lowered eyes)* I think I can figger that out about what half the daughters in the world would want. She wants to make a home for you. And to give up her life for you.

(She goes out with the service table.)

WALBECK. *(softly)* Good God – (**BERNICE** *returns and stands at the door.*) She's seventeen! How could she get such an idea! Her mother must have told her what she thought of me told her every day for eight years what she thought of me –

BERNICE. *(always without looking at him, broodingly)* Yes. *(slight pause)* Mr. Walbeck, you ought to know that women don't believe what women say. Least of all their mothers. They'll believe any old fool thing a man says.

WALBECK. She's seventeen! How did she do it? How did she get away from her mother? She must have run away at the railway station. She probably has very little money.

BERNICE. *("seeing" it; staring before her)* She's got some rings, hasn't she? She'll be selling them. She'll be going to the stores hunting for a job.

WALBECK. *(staring at her)* Yes. – But her mother will have come back to look for her. Or will have telephoned the police to look for her.

BERNICE. Maybe not. Maybe not at all…It's terrible when young girls are brave.

WALBECK. *(In a sort of terror. For the first time loudly.)* Bernice! – What shall I do?

BERNICE. *(a quick glance of somber anger)* It ain't right to ask advices. It ain't right, Mr. Walbeck.

WALBECK. See here, Bernice! Do this for me.

BERNICE. Do what, for you?

WALBECK. Do what you'd do, if it were your own daughter.

BERNICE. *(sudden flood of tormented emotion)* How do I know if I did right? – What I did about my own daughter? Maybe my daughter'd be having a good big life living with me. Maybe she's just having one of them silly lives, living with silly people and saying jabber – jabber silly things all day. *(gazing before her)* I hate people who don't know that lots of people is hungry and that lots of people has done bad things. If my daughter was with me, we'd talk …I got so many things I've *learned* that I could tell to a girl like that…And we'd go downtown and we'd shop for her clothes together…and talk… I've got a weak heart; I shouldn't get excited. *(She looks at the floor a minute.)* No, Mr. Walbeck, don't ask me to throw your daughter back into the trashy lives that most people live.

WALBECK. When she comes, give her her choice. I'll go upstairs.

BERNICE. Young people can't make choices. They don't know what they're choosing.

WALBECK. *(with increasing almost choked urgency)* Then tell her…she and I'll go away together. Somewhere. We'll start a new life.

*(***BERNICE*** is silent a moment. Then her mood changes. For the first time she brings a long deep gaze toward him.)*

BERNICE. No! – These are just fancies. We're a stone around their necks now! If we were with them we'd be a bigger stone. Sometimes I think death come into the world so we wouldn't *be* a stone around young people's necks. Besides you and I – we're alone. We did what we did because we were that kind of person – the kind that chooses to think they're smarter and better than other people…And people that think that way end up alone. We're not *company* for anybody.

*(Pause. **WALBECK**'s mood also changes.)*

WALBECK. *(his mind made up)* Then tell her that the doctors told me that I had only a few months to live…that I've gone off so as not to be a weight on anybody…on her, for instance. *(He pulls the envelope from his pocket.)* If she's not followed her mother to California, she'll be needing some money. Give her this envelope. *(his tormented urgency returns)* And tell her…Tell her…

BERNICE. *(somberly but largely)* I knows what else to tell her, Mr. Walbeck. You go upstairs and hide youself. You's almost dead. You's dyin'.

*(**WALBECK** goes out. **BERNICE** sits in a chair facing the audience, waiting, her eyes on the distance.)*

End of Play

 THORNTON WILDER (1897-1975) was an accomplished novelist and playwright whose works explore the connection between the commonplace and the cosmic dimensions of human experience. He won three Pulitzer Prizes: for his novel *The Bridge of San Luis Rey*, and two plays, *Our Town* and *The Skin of Our Teeth*. Wilder's farce, *The Matchmaker*, was adapted as the musical *Hello, Dolly!* He also enjoyed enormous success as a translator, adaptor, actor, librettist and lecturer/teacher. Wilder's many honors include the Gold Medal for Fiction from the American Academy of Arts and Letters and the Presidential Medal of Freedom. Penelope Niven's definitive biography, *Thornton Wilder: A Life*, was published in October 2012. For more information, please visit www.thorntonwilder.com.

Also by
Thornton Wilder...

The Alcestiad

The Beaux' Stratagem (with Ken Ludwig)

The Matchmaker

Our Town

The Skin of Our Teeth

<u>Thornton Wilder One Act Series: The Ages of Man</u>

Infancy

Childhood

Youth

The Rivers Under the Earth

<u>Thornton Wilder One Act Series: Wilder's Classic One Acts</u>

The Long Christmas Dinner

Queens of France

Pullman Car Hiawatha

Love and How to Cure It

Such Things Only Happen in Books

The Happy Journey to Trenton and Camden

<u>Thornton Wilder One Act Series: The Seven Deadly Sins</u>

The Drunken Sisters

Bernice

The Wreck on the 5:25

A Ringing of Doorbells

In Shakespeare and the Bible

Someone From Assisi

Cement Hands

Please visit our website **samuelfrench.com** for complete descriptions and licensing information.

www.ingramcontent.com/pod-product-compliance
Lightning Source LLC
Chambersburg PA
CBHW071419290426
44108CB00014B/1889